Leading in COLOR

LEADERSHIP LESSONS FROM THE ANIMAL WORLD

Leading IN COLOR

LEADERSHIP LESSONS FROM THE ANIMAL WORLD

ACTIVITY BOOK #1

Animals on Land

WRITTEN BY

JENNIFER REISER

ILLUSTRATED BY

SHANNON GROSS

INTRODUCTION BY DAVE NORDEL, CMSgt, USAF (RET.)

Leading in Color: Leadership Lessons from the Animal World
(Activity Book 1, Animals on Land)
Published by Rise Up Leadership Media
Billings, Montana, U.S.A.

REISER, JENNIFER, Author
LEADING IN COLOR (Book 1)
JENNIFER REISER

Library of Congress Control Number: 2023915145

ISBN: 979-8-9888453-0-0 , 979-8-9888453-1-7 (paperback)
ISBN: 979-8-9888453-4-8 (digital)

BUSINESS & ECONOMICS / Leadership
PSYCHOLOGY / Animal & Comparative Psychology
GAMES & ACTIVITIES / Activity Books

Illustration & Book Design: Shannon Gross (studioone44.com)
Publishing Management: Susie Schaefer (finishthebookpublishing.com)

QUANTITY PURCHASES: Schools, companies, professional groups, clubs,
and other organizations may qualify for special terms when ordering quantities of this title.
For information, email jenniferreiserconsulting@gmail.com.

Dedication

To the leaders of the past, whose wisdom lights our path, to the leaders of the present, whose courage shapes our world, and to the leaders of the future, whose potential knows no bounds.

May we honor the legacies of those who came before us, drawing inspiration from their resilience and vision. May we stand alongside the leaders of today, in pursuit of progress and innovation. And may we nurture and empower the leaders of tomorrow, guiding them as they chart new horizons and transform our tomorrows.

This book is a tribute to the timeless spirit of leadership, drawing inspiration from the everyday experiences that shape our lives, and the remarkable examples of leadership found in the animal world.

Table of Contents

Introduction

Leadership is fundamental to human progress, serving as the bedrock for thriving societies. Cultivating leaders is a complex yet essential endeavor, demanding commitment, enthusiasm, and the right tools. This leadership activity book, designed for the next generation of leaders, offers a unique and enjoyable method to explore leadership through nature's lens.

Jennifer Reiser, a fervent advocate for growth and development, has brought this project to life. Her passion for leadership development and her belief in nurturing tomorrow's leaders through people development today is evident on every page. Having witnessed Jennifer's dedication and the journey of this creation, I can attest to the invaluable lessons embedded in these pages. As you embark on this fun, learning, and discovery journey, you'll experience a comprehensive view of Jennifer's expertise, passion, and love for leadership development.

Leaders today face myriad challenges, including the relentless pace of life and the demands of technology and schedules. There's a yearning to slow down, find calm, and experience benefits that improve mindfulness, emotional health, and physical well-being. Coloring, a simple yet potent tool, addresses this need. It's been shown to reduce stress, promote mindfulness, and enhance focus and concentration. Dr. Catherine Carey Levisay, a clinical psychologist, highlights its cognitive benefits, noting how coloring engages both brain hemispheres, enhancing cognitive function and memory. Dr. Joel Pearson, a cognitive neuroscientist, concurs, recognizing coloring's dual benefits of cognitive enhancement and relaxation.

This activity book utilizes nature and its creatures as metaphors for leadership traits. Nature, the ultimate equalizer, offers profound lessons through its creatures. From the elephant's wisdom to the eagle's enchantment, nature's insights into leadership are boundless.

Coloring also serves as a form of self-care, boosting emotional stability, self-esteem, and creativity. Dr. Brené Brown, a renowned research professor, asserts that coloring aids emotion management and resilience building. It encourages present-moment focus and mindfulness, leading to better emotional regulation. Leaders, in particular, can benefit from coloring's stress-reducing and clarity-enhancing properties. Dr. Emma Seppälä and Dr. Dzung X. Vo emphasize its role in stress management, decision-making, communication skill enhancement, and resilience.

This book is more than just an activity; it's an immersive experience designed to foster leadership growth. It offers a reprieve from the fast-paced world, creating a serene space conducive to learning and development. As you journey with our animals, they reveal secrets to effective leadership.

Developing leaders is a pivotal task that necessitates diverse tools. This book is one such instrument, inviting exploration and growth. Jennifer Reiser's influence is palpable throughout, making this journey not just about leadership development but also a testament to her dedication and expertise in this field. Embrace this opportunity to learn, grow, and lead in color.

—Dave Nordel, CMSgt, USAF (Ret.)

Polar Bear

Leading with
courage + patience

The Polar Bear, a majestic creature of the Arctic, embodies leadership traits that are both powerful and inspiring. Its commanding presence and strong sense of responsibility exemplify the quality of courage. As apex predators, Polar Bears are fearless hunters. They rely on their courage to approach large prey such as seals, often risking dangerous encounters on thin ice or in freezing waters

Influential leaders courageously face difficult decisions and challenges, instilling confidence and resilience within their teams. Leaders must navigate through challenging and unpredictable circumstances with both bravery and composure.

Describe a difficult decision you had to make or a challenge you faced.

_____

_____

How did you share the decision-making process with your team?

_____

_____

What can you do to increase your own self-confidence and display it to others?

_____

_____

The Polar Bear symbolizes the trait of patience. Witnessing its deliberate and strategic approach to hunting demonstrates the importance of waiting for the right moment.

Similarly, patient leaders understand the value of timing, allowing projects and plans to develop organically while providing guidance and support. Courageous leaders maintain a positive attitude and maintain a spirit of curiosity.

How do you keep a positive attitude in difficult times? Do you believe in the phrase "fake it until you make it"?

_____

_____

_____

To effectively guide and support others you must first lead yourself. How do you stay motivated?

_____

_____

_____

# Ant

The tiny yet remarkable Ant possesses truly unique leadership traits. Its strong work ethic and incredible teamwork exemplify the characteristic of determination. Ants tirelessly gather food and build intricate colonies.

Leaders demonstrate dedication and commitment to achieving shared goals. They lead by example, inspiring their team to work hard and contribute their best efforts.

Give an example of a time you led by example or modeled the behavior you wanted to see.

_____

_____

What was the outcome? Did others follow?

_____

_____

What do you do when others don't learn from your example?

_____

_____

The Ant's ability to communicate and cooperate with other Ants symbolizes the leadership trait of collaboration. Ants work harmoniously, sharing information and coordinating their efforts to accomplish complex tasks.

Similarly, collaborative leaders foster a culture of open communication, encourage teamwork, and empower individuals to contribute their unique skills for the team's collective success.

How do you encourage teamwork and empower team members?

_____

_____

What is one thing you can do in the next week to improve your internal communications?

_____

_____

What does it look like to you to work "harmoniously"?

_____

_____

Kangaroo

The Kangaroo, an iconic marsupial, exhibits truly captivating leadership traits. With its strength and protective nature, it exemplifies the trait of responsibility. Female Kangaroos carry their young in their pouches, providing warmth, protection, and nourishment until they are old enough to survive on their own.

Effective leaders take responsibility for the well-being and development of their team members.

How do you invest in your team? What more could you do?

_____

_____

How do you identify individual team members' needs and work to align them with the needs of your organization?

_____

_____

The Kangaroo's exceptional jumping ability represents the trait of agility. Their powerful leaps allow them to swiftly traverse the landscape, evading predators and reaching new heights.

Likewise, agile leaders quickly adapt to changing market conditions, seize opportunities, and guide their teams toward innovation and growth. They adapt to the changing external pressures facing the organization and adjust their management style to address changing situations.

How quickly do you adapt to change?

_____

_____

Do you thrive in chaos or order? How does that compare to those you lead?

_____

_____

Describe a time you lead your team through change. How did you consider other people's concerns during this time?

_____

_____

Were you successful? If yes, how did you celebrate? If not, what would you change?

_____

_____

Cheetah

The Cheetah, a magnificent and swift predator, embodies leadership traits that are both captivating and powerful. With its unmatched speed and focus, it exemplifies the traits of determination, confidence, and fearlessness.

The Cheetah is relentless; effective leaders display unwavering determination in pursuing their goals. They inspire their team members to strive for excellence, maintain focus, and persistently work towards achieving outstanding results.

How can you embody the spirit of the Cheetah, harnessing your confidence and adaptability in your pursuit of success?

_____

_____

How and when do you set goals?

_____

_____

How often do you check in with your team as to their progress with these goals?

_____

_____

How do you motivate your team to keep them focused on the goals?

_____

_____

Furthermore, the Cheetah's exceptional vision and strategic hunting techniques represent the leadership trait of foresight, adaptability, and calculated decision making. It keenly observes its surroundings, strategizes its approach, and accurately assesses the situation.

Leaders with foresight anticipate future trends, envision possibilities, and make insightful decisions that propel their teams toward long-term success.

What do you do with an individual who is not on track?

_____

_____

Is there anything you do to help foresee potential pitfalls before they happen?

_____

_____

Grey Wolf

The Grey Wolf, a symbol of unity and strength, embodies leadership traits that command respect. Its exceptional teamwork and loyalty to the pack exemplify the quality of collaboration.

Just as wolves cooperate and communicate effectively during hunts, influential leaders foster a sense of unity, encourage collaboration, and leverage the diverse strengths of their team members to achieve shared goals.

On a scale from 1 to 10, how connected is your team? _____

What do you need to improve collaboration?

_____

_____

How do you determine your strengths and those of your team members?

_____

_____

How do you communicate these strengths to the rest of the team?

_____

_____

The Grey Wolf's strong leadership within the pack highlights the trait of assertiveness. Alphas lead confidently, making decisions that benefit the pack's survival and guiding their followers with authority.

Likewise, assertive leaders exhibit a clear vision, communicate effectively, and make decisive choices that inspire trust and motivate their team.

Describe a time your team faced unease or uncertainty.

_____

_____

What difficult decisions did you have to make?

_____

_____

How did you reassure your team during this time?

_____

_____

Golden Retriever

Leading with loyalty + trust

The Golden Retriever, a beloved and loyal companion, embodies leadership traits that are both heartwarming and impactful. Its unwavering loyalty and gentle demeanor exemplify the quality of trustworthiness. The Golden Retriever's ability to empathize and provide comfort symbolizes the leadership trait of compassion. They have an innate sense of understanding and support for those in need.

Golden Retrievers form deep bonds with their human companions. Influential leaders cultivate trust within their teams, displaying integrity, honesty, and reliability, which inspires loyalty and fosters a collaborative and productive environment. Compassionate leaders genuinely care for their team members, listen attentively, and provide encouragement and support, creating a nurturing and inclusive atmosphere.

How do you exhibit compassion toward your team members?

_____

_____

In what way does your organization encourage your employees to serve in the community?

_____

_____

What changes could you make to provide more encouragement and support?

_____

_____

Golden Retriever's eagerness to please and learn represents the leadership trait of teachability. They are highly trainable and responsive to guidance and feedback.

Teachable leaders demonstrate a growth mindset, willingly seek knowledge and insights, and continuously learn and improve, inspiring their team members to do the same.

What do you do to invest in yourself?

_____

_____

_____

How do you seek feedback from your team, clients, and community?

_____

_____

_____

Honey Bee

The Honey Bee's outward appearance radiates confidence, charisma, wisdom, and strength. The delicate stripes across its abdomen represented its impeccable organization and ability to streamline tasks for the hive. A Honey Bee exhibits the leadership traits of focus and balance.

Confidence, wisdom, and strength can be leveraged for leadership success. Additionally, leaders need to remember that true strength lies in authentic leadership and finding ways to work in real, genuine, and sincere ways.

What does authentic leadership mean to you?

_____

_____

_____

Each Honey Bee has a specific job to do. They don't take on more than they can handle, and they don't have the option to delegate tasks, authority, or responsibility.

Effective leaders can use delegation to free up time to think strategically and be more productive. They can also focus on finding better ways to lead and coach their teams.

How do you know when you are spread to thin, and who can provide the support you need to avoid burnout?

_____

What do you do to disconnect from your work to refresh and rejuvenate? How do you encourage others to do the same?

_____

_____

What is one thing you wish you could delegate?

_____

_____

Who has the skills, desire, and time to assist you, and what do they need from you as a leader to be successful?

_____

_____

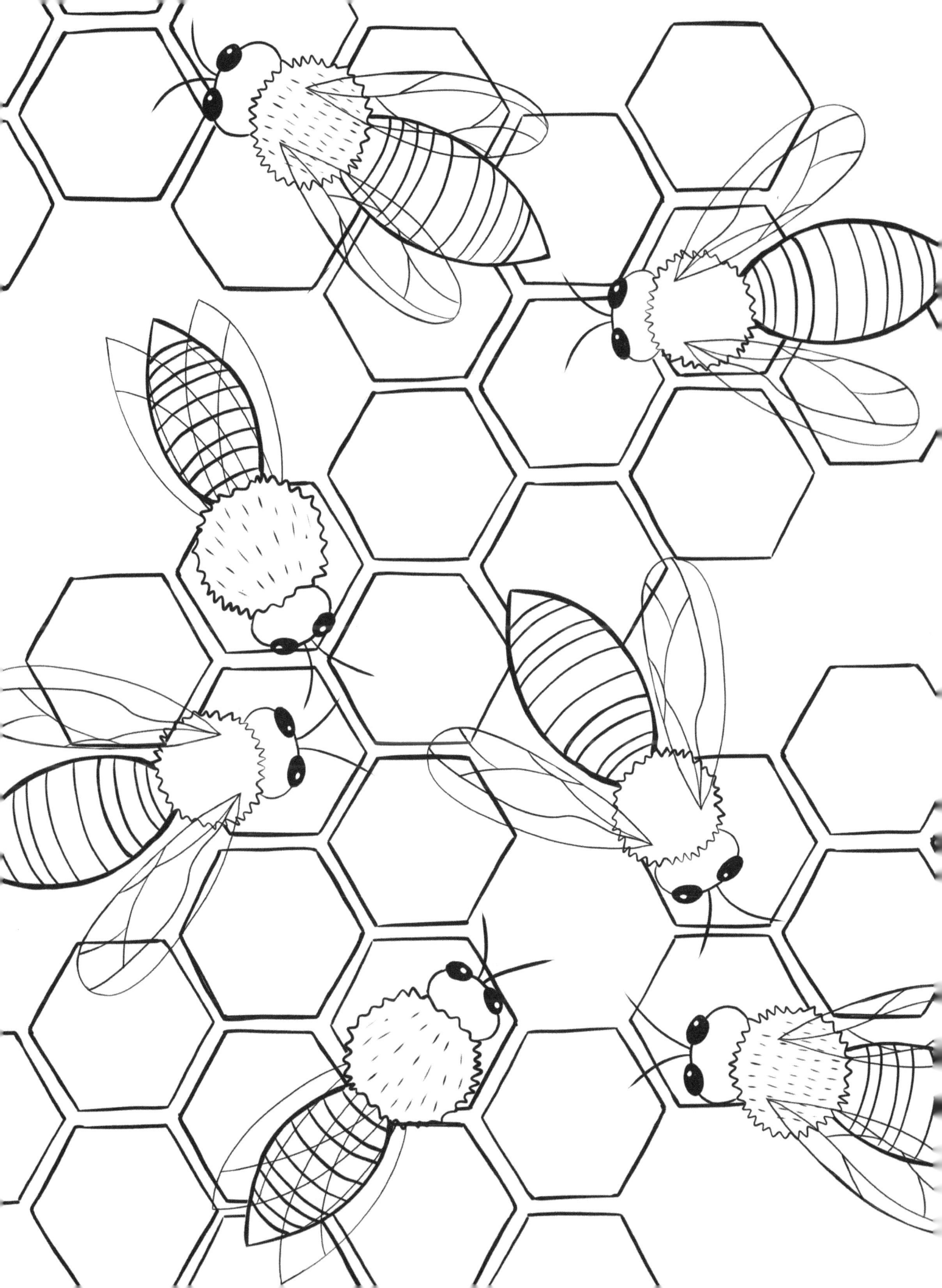

The Fox is a clever animal, and it leverages its cleverness to find innovative approaches to addressing problems, make wise decisions, and adapt to various situations effectively.

A clever leader thinks both strategically and creatively. Strategic thinking enables teams to envision both the journey and the outcome when planning. This leads to a clear set of goals, objectives, and responsibilities as well as a shared outcome.

Describe a creative problem-solving approach you have used and how it brought you success.

_____

_____

Who is the most innovative individual on your team and how do you leverage their strengths?

_____

_____

Foxes are also known for their adaptability, adjusting their approach, plans, and strategies based on changing circumstances, enabling them to stay ahead of challenges and seize opportunities.

A successful leader thinks strategically and aligns their ability to plan and execute actions effectively. When leaders use long-term vision, set clear objectives, and formulate well-thought-out plans they can better guide their teams to success.

Using good strategy, being clever, and adapting as needed makes a leader capable of navigating complex situations, inspiring their team, and achieving success in their endeavors.

How do you use strategy in your day-to-day work?

_____

_____

How do you ensure that plans and actions align with your organizational mission and long-term vision?

_____

_____

Who is the most inspirational leader you know and how can you emulate their positive traits?

_____

_____

_____

Spider

Spiders are known for their meticulous approach to building intricate webs. Spiders exemplify patience and perseverance through the time they invest in constructing their webs and waiting for prey.

As leaders, individuals with Spider-like traits excel in strategic planning. They carefully assess situations, set clear objectives, and create well-structured plans to achieve their goals. Their strategic vision helps them navigate complexities and make informed decisions.

A leader with Spider-like traits also demonstrates patience in handling challenges and setbacks. They remain determined and persistent, willing to adapt their strategies as needed while keeping their long-term objectives in focus.

Do you consider yourself a patient person? What would others say about your patience?

_____

_____

Describe a time that adaptability and perseverance paid off for you.

_____

_____

Certain Spiders, like social Spiders, exhibit cooperative behaviors. They work together to build complicated webs and collaborate on capturing prey.

A Spider-like leader values effective communication and collaboration within their team. They foster an environment of open dialogue, where ideas and feedback are welcomed. This inclusive approach promotes teamwork, strengthens relationships, and leads to increased productivity and innovation.

A Spider's web is an intricate design with many connections. Successful leaders intentionally build connections, foster relationships, and grow communities.

How do you convey a welcoming and inclusive message during your recruitment interviews and employee onboarding?

_____

_____

What is one connection, relationship, or community you are currently growing?

_____

_____

How do you encourage your team members to engage in community?

_____

_____

Lion

Lions are known as the "King of the Jungle" for their courage and strength which gives them a powerful presence.

A leader with Lion-like traits demonstrates courage in facing challenges head-on and doesn't shy away from difficult decisions. They have the strength to lead their team through adversity and inspire others with their determination and resilience.

How can you balance being a strong leader while showing compassion and empathy?

_____

_____

_____

Lions are protective of their pride and provide support to their family members. Their strong presence helps create a sense of stability and security, allowing their pride to feel supported and motivated.

Successful leaders keep one eye on the goals and another on their team, ensuring their well-being, and fostering a supportive and inclusive environment. They prioritize the growth and development of their team members, empowering them to reach their full potential.

What more can you do to grow and develop your team?

_____

_____

_____

What additional resources do you need?

_____

_____

_____

How do you individualize support for your team members?

_____

_____

_____

Gorilla

Gorillas are known for their physical strength and resilience. A mighty Gorilla reigns with both a strong physical presence and a quiet demeanor. Its intense gaze and imposing stature commands respect while also instilling calm and comfort.

A leader with Gorilla-like traits demonstrates inner strength to handle challenges and difficult situations. They remain composed and steady during times of adversity, inspiring confidence in their team and guiding them through tough times.

Successful leaders are calm in crisis and prepare to respond to challenges and difficult situations.

Compare and contrast a time you faced a difficult situation and handled it well with one that you didn't. What was the difference between the situation, how you responded, and why?

_____

_____

_____

Gorillas are protective of their group, caring for the members of their troop and exhibit empathy and emotional intelligence in their social interactions. They use both verbal and non-verbal forms of communication to relay messages, build connections, and foster a sense of unity and loyalty.

Exceptional leaders prioritize the well-being of their team, providing support, guidance, and mentorship. They create a safe and nurturing environment where team members can thrive and grow. They are also self-aware and prioritize their own well-being because they acknowledge that to be good for others they must first take care of themselves.

Check your verbal and non-verbal communications. Are they providing a consistent message to your team?

_____

_____

_____

List the top 10 things on your to-do list. Where do YOU fit on the list? How can you better prioritize your personal wellbeing?

_____

_____

_____

Elephant

Elephants command respect with their imposing presence and assertive behavior. They are also known for their wisdom and long memory, which they use to navigate their environment and make informed decisions.

A leader with Elephant-like traits exudes a strong leadership presence that inspires confidence and trust in their team. Their calm and composed demeanor fosters a sense of stability and security among their followers.

How does your leadership style change in times of challenge or crisis?

_____

_____

Effective leaders possess wisdom gained from experience and use it to guide their team effectively. They draw from past successes and challenges to make wise choices for the future.

Whether you've been a leader for 5 months, 5 years, or 5 decades, you have unique experiences. Describe a past success or challenge and how it continues to influence you.

_____

_____

Elephants are highly social animals that exhibit strong bonds and empathetic behavior towards members of their herds. Elephants within a herd engage in various social interactions, such as grooming, playing, and sharing resources. They communicate through vocalizations, body language, and tactile interactions, reinforcing their social connections.

A leader with emotional intelligence readily shows empathy and compassion towards their team. They genuinely care about the well-being of their team members, understanding their needs, and providing support and encouragement. This can lead to better relationships, as well as provide insight into how to best engage with individuals, leverage their strengths and assign responsibilities.

How do you seek to understand the needs of your team members?

_____

_____

How engaged are you with your team? Where can you do better?

_____

_____

African Wild Dog

Leading with
collaboration + coordination

African Wild Dogs are exceptional at teamwork and collaboration. They live and hunt in highly coordinated packs, where each member has a specific role to play. African Wild Dogs are known for their adaptability in dynamic environments and adjust their hunting strategies based on the circumstances they face.

A leader with African Wild Dog-like traits values collaboration within their team, encourages open communication, and leverages the diverse strengths of their team members to achieve common goals. Failure to work collaboratively can stifle innovation, lower employee morale, and result in wasted resources.

What project are you currently working on that could benefit from new collaboration?

_____

_____

Who possesses what you need? If you don't know, who can you ask?

_____

_____

African Wild Dogs employ strategic thinking and coordinated efforts during hunts. They have keen instincts and rely on their physical speed as well as their large, round ears for success.

Perceptive leaders employ active listening and learn to trust their instincts. They analyze situations critically, consider potential outcomes, and act decisively when necessary.

Describe a time that you ignored your instincts when you should have listened to them. What was the outcome? How could the outcome have been different had you trusted your instincts?

_____

_____

How does your team collaborate with external partners for success?

_____

_____

What are the written and unwritten "rules" or "boundaries" for these partnerships? What should they be?

_____

_____

Squirrel

Leading with
resourcefulness +
persistence

Squirrels are adaptable, agile, quick, and efficient animals that exhibit the traits of resourcefulness and planning. They are known for their resourcefulness in gathering and storing food for the future and making the most of their available resources.

Effective financial planning is a key aspect of resourcefulness. Leaders who can manage budgets and allocate funds strategically demonstrate their ability to maximize available resources.

Review your budgeting process and timeline. What changes can you make to maximize your resources (e.g., people, time, money)?

_____

_____

Efficient use of time is a crucial resource. A resourceful leader prioritizes tasks, delegates effectively, and avoids wasting time on non-essential activities.

Identify three tasks you'd like to delegate.

_____

_____

Who can take those tasks and what do they need to be successful?

_____

_____

Squirrels exhibit persistence in their efforts to secure food and build nests. Through continuous effort, they persistently search for food, even in challenging conditions. They tirelessly hop from tree to tree, dig through leaves and debris, and explore various locations until they find the sustenance they need.

A leader demonstrates persistence by consistently and tenaciously pursuing goals, overcoming obstacles, and maintaining a positive attitude despite challenges. Success comes when leaders persistently motivate their teams and dedicate themselves to tasks committed to achieving set goals and objectives.

What motivates you?

_____

_____

Why did you become a leader?

_____

_____

Red Panda

Red Pandas are known for their playful and joyful behavior which involves a combination of physical activities, social interactions, and exploration. Red Pandas engage in various forms of physical play, such as chasing their own tails, rolling around, leaping, and running in a playful manner. These behaviors mimic the playfulness of juvenile animals and convey a sense of joy.

A leader with Red Panda-like traits maintains a positive attitude and encourages a fun and collaborative work environment. Their approachability and humor create a more enjoyable atmosphere for their team.

How does your team have fun at work?

_____

_____

What do you do to celebrate your accomplishments?

_____

_____

When was the last time you celebrated with your team? How can you do this more often?

_____

_____

Red Pandas demonstrate curiosity by exploring their surroundings. They may investigate new objects, scents, or locations, showing their enthusiasm for discovering the world around them. They are resourceful animals and utilize their surroundings to their advantage.

Review the physical environment of your workplace. How can you improve and better utilize your surroundings?

_____

_____

_____

What could you change to encourage more social connection, physical activity, and fun?

_____

_____

_____

Hyena

Leading with
self-dominance, aggression, +
divisiveness

Hyenas exhibit a hierarchical structure where dominant individuals assert their authority selfishly, often leading to conflict and minimal collaboration within the group. Additionally, Hyenas resort to aggression and bullying to establish dominance, often targeting weaker members of the group.

Poor leaders within organizations often prioritize their personal interests over the team's well-being. They undermine collaboration, suppress diverse perspectives, and create a toxic atmosphere that stifles innovation. Additionally aggressive tactics and bullying may lead to hostile environments, undermine morale, and negatively impact team cohesion and productivity.

How do you set aside your individual professional goals for the betterment of your team/organization?

_____

_____

What can you do to encourage diverse perspectives and foster a sense of team cohesion?

_____

_____

Hyena groups are often divided, with infighting and power struggles leading to a lack of unity. Leaders must watch for signs of divisiveness within their teams, recognizing early warning signs of lack of team cohesion. When team members are pitted against one another, factions are created, and cooperation is discouraged. This leads to eroding trust and prevents the team from working harmoniously.

List five signs of a toxic work environment and strategies you can use to address them.

1. _____

_____

2. _____

_____

3. _____

_____

4. _____

_____

5. _____

_____

 Bison

Bison live in herds, working together as they graze, migrate, and defend against predators. They exhibit a strong sense of unity and cooperation within their group. Bison herds are led by the older, more experienced members who make decisions for the group. However, the input of various members is considered before making essential choices.

Effective leaders foster a sense of unity among their team members. They encourage collaboration, open communication, and a shared sense of purpose. Just as Bison work together for the collective benefit of the herd, great leaders promote teamwork to achieve common goals.

What systems does your organization have in place to promote unity and a sense of belonging among employees?

_____

_____

_____

How do your policies and procedures reflect these practices?

_____

_____

_____

Effective leaders value input from all team members and seek diverse perspectives when making decisions. They understand that inclusive decision-making results in more well-rounded choices and empowers team members to contribute their expertise.

How does your organization promote multi-generational collaboration and idea sharing?

_____

_____

_____

How do you recruit and hire with diverse perspectives in mind?

_____

_____

_____

What more can you do?

_____

_____

_____

Meerkat

Meerkats take turns being sentinels, standing guard to protect the group from potential threats while others forage. Meerkats exhibit collaborative teamwork as they live in tight-knit groups and work together to search for food, care for their young, and protect each other from predators.

Effective leaders take on the role of protecting their team from potential risks and challenges. They are vigilant about identifying and addressing issues that could hinder progress, ensuring the team's overall safety and success.

How does your organization identify and assess potential risks, both internal and external, that could impact its operations and objectives?

_____

_____

What measures and strategies have you implemented to mitigate or manage identified risks effectively, and how do you prioritize them?

_____

_____

Meerkats adapt to changes in their environment and are resourceful in finding food and shelter, even in challenging conditions.

Effective leaders exhibit adaptability and resourcefulness when faced with obstacles. They guide their team in navigating change, finding creative solutions, and turning challenges into opportunities for growth. Adaptability is a valuable quality in leaders, as it involves the ability to find creative solutions to problems and make the most of available resources.

Share an example from your leadership experience where adaptability played a critical role in overcoming a significant challenge or achieving a specific goal.

_____

_____

_____

How do you foster a culture of adaptability within your team or organization, and what strategies do you use to encourage employees to think creatively and make the most of available resources?

_____

_____

_____

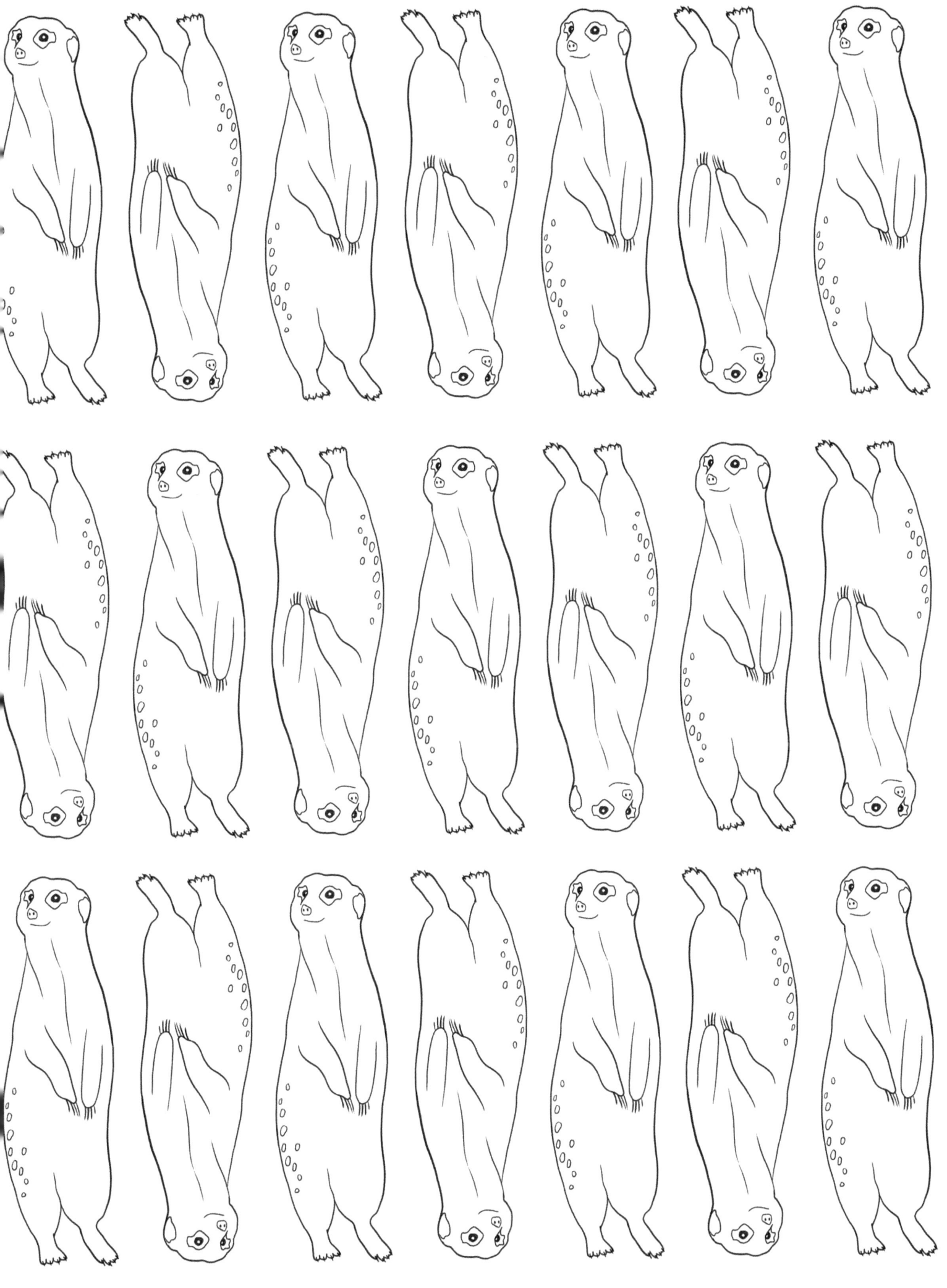

Horse

Horses are highly attuned to the emotions of other Horses and humans, sensing fear, anxiety, or calmness through subtle cues. This is due to their natural instincts and keen observational skills. Horses are known for their empathy. They can sense when someone is feeling sad, happy, or calm. In some cases, Horses may be drawn to people who are emotionally distressed and may offer comfort through their presence and gentle interactions.

Successful leaders possess emotional intelligence, recognizing and empathizing with their team members' emotions. This understanding helps them provide appropriate support, address concerns, and maintain a harmonious work environment.

How do you perceive the role of emotional intelligence in effective leadership, and how has it personally influenced your leadership style?

_____

_____

How do you develop your own emotional intelligence and encourage your team members to enhance their own emotional intelligence?

_____

_____

Horses establish trust and respect through consistent behaviors, creating a hierarchy within their herd based on mutual understanding and cooperation. Additionally, within a Horse herd, dominant, trusted Horses lead by example, showcasing desired behaviors and guiding the group's actions.

Effective leaders prioritize building trust and respect within their team. They demonstrate reliability, consistency, and integrity, fostering a positive atmosphere where team members feel valued and supported. Effective leaders lead by example, demonstrating the values, work ethic, and behaviors they expect from their team members. This practice sets a positive tone, influences behavior, and creates a culture of high standards.

How do you establish and nurture trust within your team or organization, particularly in times of change or uncertainty? How does this differ with your stakeholders?

_____

_____

How do you address trust issues or breaches when they occur, and what steps do you take to rebuild trust with your team or stakeholders?

_____

_____

Raccoon

Raccoons exhibit curiosity and engage in complex problem-solving, using their intelligence to explore and manipulate their environment. They utilize a wide range of environments and food sources to thrive.

Curious leaders promote a culture of curiosity and critical thinking within their team. They encourage team members to ask questions, seek solutions, and approach tasks with an open, inquisitive mindset. Leading by example and providing learning opportunities are keys to successfully creating an environment where asking questions is welcomed and encouraged.

How do you demonstrate curiosity in your own work and decision-making?

_____

_____

What can you do to be more open to new ideas, perspectives, and feedback?

_____

_____

How do you encourage your team to think differently and approach problems from multiples angles?

_____

_____

Raccoons exhibit caution and carefully assess their surroundings before taking risks, weighing potential benefits against potential dangers. They are nocturnal creatures, adapting to the challenges and opportunities presented by both nighttime and daytime environments.

Positive leaders show adaptability and resilience in various situations. They guide their team through different phases of projects or challenges, providing support and guidance regardless of the circumstances. Effective leaders encourage calculated risk-taking and provide guidance for decision-making. They help their team members evaluate risks, making informed choices that align with organizational goals.

How do you evaluate risks before taking on new projects? How do you continue to integrate evaluation throughout the life cycle of a project?

_____

_____

How do you leverage data and analytics to assess risk based on historical trends, current market conditions, and other relevant factors? Where do you get this information?

_____

_____

Camel

Camels conserve water by minimizing sweat loss and efficiently utilizing their stored fat for energy, reflecting their mastery of resource conservation. Camels cover vast distances over extended periods, conserving energy and demonstrating their ability to focus on reaching distant destinations.

Successful leaders manage resources strategically, ensuring the optimal use of time, talents, and materials. They guide their team to prioritize tasks, avoid burnout, and achieve sustainable success without wastefulness.

Strategic resource management includes establishing clear priorities and goals, clear communications, and working collaboratively. Additionally, regularly reassessing and reprioritizing tasks based on changing circumstances, feedback, or new information are keys to success.

How do you clearly communicate organizational priorities and goals to the team?

_____

How do you ensure that everyone understands the overarching objectives and how their individual tasks contribute to the larger mission?

_____

How do you encourage flexibility and adaptability in response to evolving priorities?

_____

Endurance is crucial for leaders as it enables them to persevere through challenges, drive longterm goals, and inspire resilience within their teams. However, leaders must balance endurance with self-care and encourage their teams to prioritize personal well-being and manage stress.

How do you encourage employees to maintain a healthy work-life balance by setting realistic expectations for workload and deadlines?

_____

_____

How do you acknowledge the importance of personal time and self-care and demonstrate your commitment to work-life balance?

_____

_____

What policies do you have in place to support a more sustainable and balanced work environment (e.g. flexible work arrangements, remote work options, compressed workweeks, etc.)?

_____

_____

Sloth

Sloths exhibit a slow-paced lifestyle, emphasizing patience and thoughtfulness in their actions and decisions.

Effective leaders demonstrate patience and thoughtfulness in their leadership approach. They take time to consider options, listen to various perspectives, and make well-informed decisions that benefit the team and organization.

Reflect on your recent decisions and interactions with team members. Consider whether you approached situations with patience or if impatience influenced your actions.

_____

_____

_____

Do you allow time for thoughtful reflection? Assess whether impatience or the desire for quick solutions hinders your ability to respond thoughtfully.

_____

_____

_____

Sloths live a peaceful and balanced life, valuing tranquility and harmony in their interactions with their environment. Sloths move slowly and gently through their surroundings, reflecting a leadership style that is considerate and gentle in interactions.

Effective leaders create a peaceful work environment that promotes well-being and balance. They recognize the importance of providing a calm atmosphere where team members can focus, innovate, and thrive.

Think about recent situations where decisions were made, or conflicts arose. Reflect on how thoroughly you considered different perspectives before making a judgment. Did you take the time to understand varying viewpoints and how did it influence your thoughtfulness in decision-making?

_____

_____

_____

How do you create harmony and foster an environment where team members can work at their own pace while maintaining a collaborative atmosphere that supports mutual understanding?

_____

_____

_____

Badger

Badgers are known for their persistence and determination when it comes to digging and burrowing. They are also known for their fierce protection of their territory and young and can be bold defenders when threatened. Badgers exhibit a relentless pursuit of their goals.

Leaders can cultivate persistence by staying focused on long-term objectives, overcoming setbacks, and demonstrating resilience in the face of challenges. This involves maintaining a strong work ethic and encouraging the team to persevere through difficulties.

How do you respond to setbacks and challenges? Explore whether setbacks discourage you or if you view them as opportunities to learn and persist.

_____

_____

_____

What do you do to maintain a focus on long-term goals amidst daily pressures and unanticipated challenges? How well do you balance immediate needs with the pursuit of long-term goals?

_____

_____

_____

When hunting, Badgers display tenacity by patiently waiting near the entrance of a burrow or a rodent hole. They can wait for extended periods, showing remarkable patience until their prey emerges. Once the opportunity arises, Badgers swiftly and persistently pursue and capture their prey. This hunting strategy showcases their ability to persistently wait for the right moment and then act with tenacity to secure their food source.

Leading with tenacity means being the kind of person who never gives up and never stops trying, doing whatever is required to accomplish a goal. However, tenacity taken too far may turn into stubbornness. Knowing when to pause, reassess, and adapt is essential to leadership success.

How do you maintain a balance between tenacity and adaptability in your leadership approach? Consider situations where adjustments were needed in your plans and assess how well you maintained your determination while adapting to new circumstances.

_____

_____

_____

Chameleon

Chameleons are renowned for their adaptability, changing color to blend into their environment and adjusting to different conditions. Chameleons have keen observation skills and heightened situational awareness, enabling them to readily detect changes in their surroundings.

Adaptability is a crucial quality for leaders in today's dynamic and ever-changing work environments. Leaders can learn the importance of adaptability by being open to change, embracing new ideas, and adjusting strategies in response to evolving circumstances. Being flexible allows leaders to navigate uncertainties and lead their teams effectively in dynamic environments.

To what extent do you embrace change as an opportunity for growth and improvement? In what situations do you tend to resist change?

_____

_____

In what ways do you encourage adaptability within your team? What support, resources, and encouragement do you provide when facing unexpected challenges?

_____

_____

Chameleons use color changes as a means of communication, conveying emotions, intentions, or responses to stimuli.

Strategic communication is essential for effective leadership. Clear and effective communication, both verbal and non-verbal, is crucial for conveying goals, expectations, and values. Adapting communication styles to different audiences enhances a leader's ability to connect with and influence their team.

What do you consider when developing your approach to communicating with various stakeholders, including team members, superiors, and external partners?

_____

_____

How do you tailor your communication style to suit different audiences?

_____

_____

In what situations, or with what audiences, do you need to be more adaptable?

_____

_____

ABOUT THE AUTHOR

A multifaceted professional with expertise in cultivating networks, Jennifer Reiser fosters growth at individual and community levels, excelling in organization management and leadership development. She is the CEO and founder of Jennifer Reiser Consulting and has decades of nonprofit and organizational management experience.

Jennifer values productivity, efficiency, and dependability, and is intrigued by the unique qualities of each person. She has a gift for discovering how different people can work together productively. Jennifer is committed to developing individuals, building teams, and creating communities where people can not only be themselves, but grow to be someone they never thought they could be.

Fascinated with books, Jennifer has always dreamed of being an author. With a passion for travel and people, she lives life as both an active observer and passionate connector. She draws from her relationships with strong, seasoned leaders as well as emerging leaders, and strives to meet people where they are to encourage their individual development.

Jennifer is the mother of two amazing daughters that have taught her the importance of being yourself, celebrating differences, and supporting each other's hopes and dreams. Jennifer has roots in Wisconsin and lives in Montana, inspiring others to create learning opportunities, cultivate new experiences, and celebrate all that life has to offer.

To contact Jennifer for consulting services, email jenniferreiserconsulting@gmail.com